Cesar Chavez

By Susan Eddy

Consultant
Jeanne Clidas, Ph.D.
National Reading Consultant
and
Professor of Reading, SUNY Brockport

CP Children's Press ®
A Division of Scholastic Inc.
New York Toronto London Auckland Sydney
Mexico City New Delhi Hong Kong
Danbury, Connecticut

Designer: Herman Adler Design
Photo Researcher: Caroline Anderson
The photo on the cover shows Cesar Chavez.

Library of Congress Cataloging-in-Publication Data
Eddy, Susan.
  Cesar Chavez / by Susan Eddy ; consultant, Jeanne Clidas.
      p. cm. — (Rookie biography)
Summary: A brief biography of Cesar Chavez, the Mexican American union
leader who fought to get migrant farm workers better wages.
    ISBN 0-516-25882-6 (lib. bdg.)   0-516-27923-8 (pbk.)
  1. Chavez, Cesar, 1927—Juvenile literature. 2. Labor
leaders—United States—Biography-Juvenile literature. 3. Mexican
Americans—Biography—Juvenile literature. 4. Mexican American
agricultural laborers—History—Juvenile literature. 5. Agricultural
laborers—Labor unions—United States-History—Juvenile literature.
6. United Farm Workers—History—Juvenile literature. [1. Chavez, Cesar,
1927- 2. Labor leaders. 3. Mexican Americans—Biography.] I. Title.
II. Series.
  HD6509.C48E33 2003
  331.88'13'092-dc21

                            2003004803

CHILDREN'S PRESS, and ROOKIE BIOGRAPHIES™, and associated
logos are trademarks and or registered trademarks of Scholastic Library
Publishing. SCHOLASTIC and associated logos are trademarks
and or registered trademarks of Scholastic Inc.
17 18 R 12   62

Cesar Chavez was a hero
to many people.

He spent his life working to
help others. The people he
helped were farm workers.

Most of the farm workers were
Mexican Americans.

Yuma, Arizona

Cesar Chavez was born in 1927 near Yuma, Arizona.

His family had a grocery store and a farm. Cesar was born in a little room over the grocery store.

When Cesar was ten years old,
his father had to sell the store.
Many people lost their jobs.
Two years later, his father had
to sell the farm, too.

The family went to California
to look for work.

Other people tied their furniture
(FUR-nuh-chur) to their cars
and moved away.

Cesar's family became migrant (MYE-gruhnt) farm workers. Migrant workers move from place to place looking for work.

Cotton

Tomatoes

They picked crops like cotton
and tomatoes.

A town of shacks

Cesar and his family never stayed in one place for long. They lived in shacks with one room.

Cesar left school at the end of eighth grade. He worked in the fields to help his family.

Many children had to work in the fields. This helped the family have more money.

The farm owners were not fair to the workers. The workers did all the work, but the farm owners made all the money.

Cesar knew this was not right.

Cesar wanted to change things. He traveled from farm to farm, talking to the workers.

20

He organized (OR-guh-nized) the workers into a union (YOON-yuhn).

A union is like a club. Cesar was the leader.

The union demanded fair pay and better places to live.

In 1965, the grape-pickers went on strike. They did not work until they got higher pay.

People stopped buying grapes to show their support for the workers.

The strike lasted five years.
Farm owners agreed to many
of their demands.

Cesar Chavez taught his union
that even poor people have
power when they work together.

Even after the strike was over, Cesar continued to help farm workers.

Cesar Chavez died in 1993.
The next year, President Clinton
honored Cesar by giving his
wife the Presidential Medal
of Freedom.

Words You Know

Cesar Chavez

crops

Mexican American

migrant worker

30

shack

strike

union

Index

About the Author

Susan Eddy grew up in New Jersey but has loved New York City all her life. She is an editor by profession and an avocational singer who enjoys writing nonfiction books for children. These days she divides her time between a small farm in New Jersey and a small brownstone in Greenwich Village.

Photo Credits